MW00677109

God! Please Save My Marriage

Proven Advice for Success and

Longevity in Marriage

Robert E. Flournoy, D. Min

Dante's Publishing • Atlanta, GA

DEDICATION

I am elated to dedicate my book to all of the married couples who have struggled or are currently struggling to achieve, maintain, and foster growth in their relationships. Regardless of the number of years you have been married, you are subject to the same kind of mistakes, missteps, and breakups that causes one in two couples to throw in the towel, separate and get a divorce.

Therefore, I am honored to be able to present this book, because I know that it will help you achieve love, success and longevity in your relationship. I pray that you will be blessed as you read and adhere to the suggestions outlined in *God! Please Save My Marriage.*

ACKNOWLEDGEMENTS

My wife, Diane, is my greatest supporter.You constantly made suggestions and comments before, during and at completion of the various sections of the book. *God! Please Save My Marriage* features our experience and testimony to how we made it through our marital journey. Thank you for your love, support and confidence in me. I can achieve success in all that I do.

Thanks to my children Britannia (Tan) and her husband, Dwane, and my son, Robert Jr., for your prayers and support. I really appreciate the encouragement you gave me.

I thank Cheryl Hosey, one of my students at Beulah Heights University, for her encouragement and constant reminder for me to finish this writing project.

My expressions of gratitude would be remiss if I didn't thank Prophet Benjamin Hines for his contribution to the project. You are an asset to the Body of Christ and to so many people. Thank God for you and all of the work that you do.

Finally, I have developed many relationships with many people and organizations. In so many ways, all of you have contributed to my success. Thank you.

TABLE OF CONTENTS

FOREWORD

We once heard a pastor say, "The Bible says that the two shall become one, and then we spend all our married life trying to decide which one we will become!" In *God! Please Save My Marriage*, Dr. Flournoy gives couples practical solutions to the complexities inherent in the marriage relationship as we strive to become the unit that God has designed.

The principles contained in this book have been tested throughout the forty-four years that Dr. and Mrs. Flournoy have shared their lives together, and the material will enable couples to locate the stage of their marriage, make mid-course adjustments, and navigate successfully through the pitfalls that threaten to challenge our oneness.

Pastors Billy and Dr. D'Ann Johnson
New Covenant Ministries

PREFACE

In the beginning God created a man and a woman to be joined together; so that through their union, they would multiply and replenish the earth. It was at that time the institution of marriage, between a man and woman, was ordained by God. Marriage is God's thing. For that reason alone, it should not be entered into unwisely or without counsel, but it is to be entered seriously and reverently with the intent to fulfill God's purposes. The marriage union must follow God's way or it will fail.

God! Please Save My Marriage is a chronicle of the successes and disappointments experienced by me and my wife, Diane, when we did not depend on God to help us love each other and lead us to His Divine will, as a married couple. In addition, it is also a guide that reveals the actual sequential steps of our married life that led us through 44 years of success. To the reader, we discovered that success in a marriage can be achieved only when you follow God's instructions. Through our own relationship and having counseled a number of couples in ministry, we found that difficulty occurs when couples attempt to solve problems on their own. Only God is all-knowing. He, more than anyone, knows what your relationship needs. Therefore, it is important to remember to seek Godly counsel, because what you put into your relationship is exactly what you will get out of it. Only God's way produces the right fruit.

First of all, my goal for this book is to inform couples how a relationship can be completely dismantled over trivial matters. Secondly, it provides examples to help you arrive at solutions that will turn a troubled situation around, through the application of simple suggestions that can lead to on-going marital success and satisfaction. While we realize that every relationship is different, these examples can be used in most situations. Finally, if you will simply follow the suggestions outlined here, we believe that your marriage will become a blessing to you, your family and friends and it will continue to be so for many years to come.

God! Please Save My Marriage

Proven Advice for Success and

Longevity in Marriage

CHAPTER 1
INTRODUCTION

The Purpose of This Book

God created man and woman to be fruitful, to multiply and fill the earth. The Bible reads according to Genesis 1:28:

"Then God blessed them, and God said to them, be fruitful and multiply; fill the earth and subdue it; have dominion over the fish of the sea, over the birds of the air, and over every living thing that moves on the earth".

God gave a powerful directive to the man and woman, to work collectively to fulfill His command. Unfortunately, since the beginning of time, thousands of people have missed that point. So the purpose of this book is to uncover areas where married couples may not work together and therefore their marriages ended or are on the road to ending in divorce. Couples that may have bypassed the "work collectively to fulfill His command" point could have stemmed from individuals establishing rules that satisfy him or herself versus rules that include both members of the couple. In other words, they stop going to church and avoid receiving counsel. These couples think they can solve their own marital problems. Prudent people, on the other hand, examine what God's word says about these matters when their marriages take a wrong turn. They also act wisely and yield to sound biblical teaching and counsel received, by faith, from the Word of God. That's when their new lifestyle for marriage becomes a transparent model for other troubled marriages to mirror. This new life also exemplifies the life that Jesus lived, when he was on earth.

The purpose for marriage is for life-time companionship where two people love each other, birth and raise their children together when it's medically possible, maintain a healthy relationship by living peaceably, and expressing and showing love for each other until "death do you part".

The problem with this statement is that most couples find that it is more easily said than done; especially when you don't know what is really conveyed by being in marriage. By this I mean, a tremendous number of married couples have received little to no pre-marital counseling. They went through the marriage ceremony without ever having a clear understanding of the vows they recited to each other. In their minds they are married and nothing else seems to matter. However, the marriage will naturally pass through several stages. When you are familiar with the stages of a marriage, you can avoid the pitfalls that prevent a happy, successful union.

During Stage (1) each partner tries to find out how to make things work, and seek information and advice from others to help them keep their marriage working. Stage (2) seems to be easier; since by this phase you know more about each other and should have developed ways to avoid making repeated relationship mistakes. Nevertheless, serious problems during this stage can lead to a divorce, if you do not know how to handle sensitive situations when they arise. During Stage (3) it seems though you have weathered the storms and have learned ways to solve the problems that occurred in Stages (1 – 3), yet at times you still contemplate getting a divorce. What's the problem? Problems can and will occur at any stage. However, remember that our Lord and Savior is the answer to all things and we must depend on Jesus, not a man, for every solution. Yes, there is a solution for every problem! The question is, do you really love each other enough to want to solve the problem? If both parties have an earnest desire to solve a problem, the problem can be resolved. If your partner has little to no desire to resolve a problem, then you will probably never arrive at a healthy solution. This dilemma is a primary reason that a marriage will most likely end in divorce. Stages 4 and 5 address proven ways for maintaining a healthy relationship.

Diane and I will never stop finding ways to make our marriage work. As we get older and the pace gets slower, our grand-children remind us that we are to fulfill His divine purpose on earth.

The final purpose which is outlined in chapters 4 and 5 is to encourage the reader to discover creative ways to maintain a healthy marriage. *Although there is nothing that can prevent marital problems, the good news is, there is a solution to every problem.* Most couples find joy in working things out without needing mediation; however, they still tend to panic when they cannot resolve the problem successfully. However, when circumstances reach the place where you cannot solve a problem between the two of you, seek help immediately from a competent, confidential and considerate married couple that you trust.

The purpose for marriage is for life-time companionship where two people love each other, birth and raise their children together when it's medically possible, maintain a healthy relationship by living peaceably, and expressing and showing love for each other until "death do you part".

This book is not intended to solve all the problems that you might encounter in your relationship. It only includes Diane's and my advice and solutions to problems we faced early in our own marriage. We have been married successfully for 44 years.

In the Name of Jesus let prudence prevail; so each reader may read this discourse very carefully, and use the information which is appropriate for their own marital growth and prosperity.

Organization and Guidelines

In addition to the foregoing information, the following four topics will be discussed in detail:

Statistics and Percentages
How Well Do You Know Me
Conflicts and Resolutions
Maintaining a Healthy Relationship

At the end of selected chapters, we have included a list of do's and don'ts to help you avoid saying and doing things that you could later on regret.

We suggest that you read the entire book; instead of only zooming in on topics that apply to your current situation. The Statistics and Percentages section will reveal information on the current trends in breakups, give-ups, and careless attitudes in relationships. Both the husband and wife are gifts from God and marriage should not be considered as something *"easy to get into and easier to get out of."*

In Proverbs 18:22 King Solomon writes,

"He who finds a wife finds a good thing and obtains
favor from the Lord."

After reading the entire book, find the Stage you are in your marriage and study it (i.e. Stage 1 or 3, etc.). That section will make you keenly aware of actions you are taking or should not be taking to foster a better marriage. Retrospectively, we recommend that you check to see if you are progressing or regressing with your spouse and then follow the tips. Be sure to follow the do's and don'ts section, to avoid making the same mistakes again. In addition, each section was especially written to enhance your growth by encouraging corrective action at each stage. Problems oftentimes exist because people do not know their mates well. In the "How Well Do You Know Me?" section you will discover items to consider when choosing a mate or staying in a marriage. This next section deals with conflicts and resolutions. Although it is obvious that we should know how to get along, but we usually don't. There are many walls that need to be torn down. When we learn how to remove barriers and tear down walls, such as unforgiveness, bitterness, etc., our marriages will become sweeter than ever before. This section focuses on tearing down walls.

The last section addresses a number of ways to
"Maintain a Healthy Relationship."

When Diane and I got married, I did not understand the importance of saying "Diane . . . I love you." In fact, I thought it was understood. I also thought, what's the big deal? Not to mention, I dare not say the "I love you" phrase or kiss her in public. For example, when we got married by Justice Of The Peace, we didn't kiss each other the way we really wanted to; because the Justice of the Peace was present. Of course that was a long time ago.

Today, I know how sweet and how important kisses are and take advantage of every opportunity to do so, and you will understand the importance of it as well.

Today, I rarely leave home without a kiss. Prior, I used expressions like, "You know how much I love you," or "If I didn't love you . . . I wouldn't do the things I do", not realizing how important it is to say that "I love you" and mean it. Fortunately, I started attending marriage seminars at my church. I found out that I was missing ways to express how much I love my wife, and how to be proactive in giving, saying, and doing things that are sometime simple but yet rewarding for both of us. In addition, when you learn to forget an offense, forgiveness of that offense is automatic. Both you and your companion are set free. There's nothing quite like a "make up" kiss.

Notes - Chapter 1

Notes - Chapter 1

CHAPTER 2
STATISTICS AND PERCENTAGES

Marriage is an enriching experience for most couples. Such a lifestyle offers companionship, increased security, sexual gratification, and a welcomed respite from stress of single life, the cares of this world and loneliness. Unfortunately, the single life has become so attractive in America that many couples have deemed the marriage contract as unnecessary.

Today, divorce is approached as a first alternative, rather than reconciliation. Many people resort to divorce because they feel that it was a mistake to have married in the first place or they just can no longer get along. Still others resort to divorce due to physical or emotional abuse from a partner or they simply grow apart.

Regardless of the reasons, divorce was never intended to take place. The scripture records Jesus as saying that Moses allowed divorce due to the hardness of people's heart, but it was not so from the beginning. (Mark 10:2-9) The majority of people still feel that marriage is an honorable institution ordained by God for keepsake until death. Statistics have shown the opposite. It has been frequently reported that 50 percent (or one in two) of marriages will end in divorce. Also by age 30, 75 percent of women in the United States will marry, and about half will have experienced an extramarital affair; according to the new comprehensive report on cohabitation, marriage, divorce, and remarriage released by the Centers for Disease Control and Prevention (CDC).

A recent study by the Barna Research Group states that, "11 percent of the adult population is currently divorced; and 25 percent of adults have had at least one divorce during their lifetime." Additionally, it states that many Christian couples find it difficult to continue attending church service after their marital separation. Meeting at church becomes awkward. Many find that the climate in their church is very negative as well. Therefore, separated parishioners usually move to other congregations that are either more accepting or unaware of their marital status.

Because of the aforementioned factors, many people have become sensitive to separation and divorce and have begun to lend support by expressing love to couples, offering encouragement, and praying that they work things out rather than ridiculing them for their difficulties. This is a change in traditional trends where people once thought it strange for someone to get a divorce. (In some cases in the past, the divorcee left town or moved to a new community.)

The Barna Group study also found: Variation in divorce rates by location in the United States:

In the South	27%
The Midwest	27%
The West	26%
The Northwest	19%

Married adults now divorce two-and-a-half times more than adults 20 years ago and four times as often as 50 years ago.

The Associated Press computed divorce statistics from data by the National Center for Health. It also reported that the state of Nevada had the highest divorce rate per 1,000 people in 1998. People from other states would visit Nevada, get their divorce, and return home single. "Prior to the latter decades of the 20th century, a spouse seeking divorce had to show a cause such as cruelty, incurable mental illness or adultery." Married adults now divorce two-and-a-half times more than adults 20 years ago and four times as often as 50 years ago.

The reasons for the growing divorce rate today can be derived from the following:

1. Some states offer cheaper rates
2. Dual careers conflict
3. Conflict with family responsibilities/in-laws
4. Lenient laws
5. Working apart rather than together
6. Sex before marriage
7. Adultery
8. Irreconcilable differences
9. Many other reasons

The purpose for marrying is for lifelong companionship for the rest of your life with a spouse. If there is a reason for a divorce, it should only be for immorality or death of one partner. God knew what He was doing when He put man and woman together. Furthermore, He knew that there would be challenges, but not beyond which He could fix. It's up to us to seek God and find a way to resolve our problems. Divorce is not the solution.

Lifestyles and Temptations

Most people don't think that the way we live today and the way we were raised can impact success or failure in our relationships. Lifestyle can cause a great deal of problems now and in the future. The more you know about a person's lifestyle, including what they like and dislike, the easier it will be to get along with them; (i.e.) dealing with an "element of surprise" such as discovering the true story surrounding the birth, early childhood, and adolescent years of your spouse can be challenging. It's hard to deal with an "element of surprise." Pre-marital counseling is good and it helps engaged couples to know in advance exactly what they will have to deal with.

Another example of facts, often discovered during premarital counseling is that, one spouse may have been raised in a family that likes to party and go places all of the time, while the other spouse came from a family who are homebodies and do family things together, as well as attend church. Or perhaps, one or both spouses came from a family who depended on the mom for everything from organizing events, writing out to-do lists to giving instructions for taking care of business. In some cases the parent(s) of the spouse(s) was doctor, counselor and the family overseer. In fact, your potential spouse may be product of a one-parent household, with a whole set of other issues.

What about eating habits, taking care of the house, cleaning up your room, getting along with siblings? These are just a few areas of potential conflict when considering a marriage partner:

1). Upbringing - performing household chores. I had chores to perform. My task was to wash dishes, carry out the trash, clean-up my room and make up my bed before leaving for school.

2). I had to help keep the house clean and do other things requested by my parents. These tasks were not everyday chores because I had two older brothers and my sister; we all shared in keeping the house clean and in order.

Some people that I knew, during my early childhood years, had to work on their family farms, take care of their younger sister(s) or brother(s), as well as feed, supervise or baby-sit them until a parent or older sibling returned home. I am sure you can concur with me in imagining the amount of problems that can arise from living with someone who had the level of responsibility of taking care of the house like you or I did. Some parents did it all and did not let the children do anything. Imagine a spouse who will not help with house work, because he or she never had to do it. In addition, let's consider those individuals fortunate enough to have had a nanny or maid service growing up. Not everyone was fortunate to afford such luxury of a maid; however I understand some spouses may have had that experience. They, too, would exhibit behavior similar to those spouses whose parents did everything for them. Regardless of the way you and your spouse were raised, it is to your benefit to be willing to make "user friendly" accommodations to include the way your mate is accustomed to living.

Let's talk about temptation . . . what about it? Paul writes,

"No temptation has overtaken you except such as is common to man; but God is faithful, who will not allow you to be tempted beyond what you are able, but with the temptation will also make the way of escape, that you may be able to bear it" (1 Corinthians 10:13).

God has provided a way of escape for all of us whenever temptation comes. Jesus was tempted and said that we would be tempted also. The problem with many people is that they don't want to escape. If you really do not want to yield to temptation, God will provide the way to get out of it and/or prevent you from doing it. We must continue to trust Him at all times when we encounter temptation. If you think that you can't be tempted, you are making a sad mistake and you are fooling yourself. Satan and all of his cohorts are well trained ancient foes. In other words, the devil knows how to out-play the "playa." There are so many ways the devil lures us into situations just to see how we will respond. The manner in which we respond or not respond to his invitations, lets him know and others know whether we will yield to the invitation. We can respond like Joseph who told Potiphar's wife, "How can I do this great wickedness and sin against God (Genesis 39:9). If we can model Joseph, who at the time didn't even have the Holy Spirit, we can resist the devil, and he will flee. Hallelujah!

Life Expectancy

In 2008, the Centers for Disease Control and Prevention (CDC) said that the United States life expectancy had increased to 78 years. Recently, the CDC changed how it calculates life expectancy, which caused a shrink in estimates to below 78. The United States continues to fall behind 30 other countries in life expectancy increase. For example, Japan has the longest life expectancy of 83 years for children born in 2007, according to the World Health Organization. There are several reasons for the increase in life expectancy in the United States: (1) HIV death rate dropped 10 percent; and (2) diabetes death rate fell 4 percent, allowing Alzheimer's disease to surpass diabetes to become the sixth leading cause of death. There are several other reasons life expectancy in the United States has increased, but these two factors stand out among others.

These statistics are proof that we are living longer. There-fore, people who are married spend more time with a com-panion and live healthier, longer lives than singles, according to research. In addition, healthy food preparation, eating and drinking in moderation, weight control and exercise are among leading reasons for our increased longevity.

As we get older, most people realize that they cannot eat the types of foods they ate when they were younger. In fact, my wife and I, years ago, started decreasing the amount of salt used in our food. Some people sit down to eat at home or at a restaurant and sprinkle salt on food before tasting it. Most foods are seasoned enough without using additional seasoning. Always taste the food before you season it. (Use of sodium is a cause of high-blood pressure, especially among African Ameri-cans.)

Fried foods, alcoholic beverages, smoking and the use of drugs are major contributors to a shorter life span. These types of habits must be overcome to live longer. The Bible records a healthy use of wine. Paul writes, *"No longer drink only water, but use a little wine for your stomach's sake and your frequent infirmi-ties"* (1 Timothy 5:23). Wise men don't drink at all. If you have never started drinking, don't. Everyone does not have self con-trol. Play it safe and don't drink at all . . . and definitely don't drink and drive! My friend, you will live longer and be around to enjoy your companion.

All of us can learn how to prepare healthier and tastier meals that are free from so many of the ingredients that are harmful to our health, like excess sugar, fat and sodium. Some ingredi-ents make the food taste good but are not good for the body. Remember, it's not always what you prepare that's so good for you. Instead, it's how you prepare it that will help to live longer.

Finally, the best way to increase your life span with your spouse is to start living, eating, and doing what is right. Eating is only one of the factors that will make us live longer and healthier. Exercise, rest, sleep, and freedom from stress give us another day to live and give thanks to the Lord for His goodness. And don't forget plain old common sense. Always remember that it's by the Grace of God that we see another moment, and by His grace we can testify... that had it not been for Him, we would not be here today.

Notes - Chapter 2

Notes - Chapter 2

CHAPTER 3
HOW WELL DO YOU KNOW ME?

Background Check

It may seem childish to have a background check done on someone you just met. In fact, parents should do it should they have doubts about the person their child is dating. Let's face it, it's for everybody's own good. How well do you know the person you're dating, if you are single? What does he or she know about you? The first time I asked my wife whether I could come to her house and see her, she said that she had to ask her mother. Instantly, her mother said yes. I thought I was really somebody special since her mother and father consented so soon to let me come and see their daughter, without knowing anything about me. However, to my surprise, her mother had checked with a neighbor who knew my mother and verified the type of family I came from, the reputation we had in the community, as well as where my parents worked. My wife's mother also knew that I was a college student and planned to become a high school teacher when I finished school. Her parents concluded that I was a handsome prospect for their daughter.

Today, there are so many cases reported of physical abuse, rape, and other threatening ways people use to gain control over people. These same people consent to marry in the midst of seeing "red flags" (wedding ring print on hand, lying, ex-spouses, criminal behavior, etc.) in their relationship while they were dating. Yet, they marry anyway! These types of precautions may seem unnecessary to some, but you must find out something about who you are going to date or marry.

This information can be obtained from the internet by search-

Today, there are so many cases reported of physical abuse, rape, and other
threatening ways people use to gain
control over people.

ing "background check". Some of the sites will ask for a small
fee and allow you to just type in the name of the person. You
will learn things you might not otherwise find out. You may be
surprised or otherwise discover that you are in good company.

How Were You Raised?

Years ago, families raised their children with morals and
strict standards according to the Holy Bible or some form of
religion. Whether the mother or the father was a Believer of the
Gospel of Jesus Christ or not, they were brought up the way
their parent's parents raised them up. The proper way to living
was passed down from generation to generation. Each generation instructed the next. King Solomon from the Bible is quoted
saying,

> *"Train up a child in the way he should go, and when he is
> old he will not depart from it" (Proverbs 22:6).*

My family, the Flournoys, was raised in a household that
was based on biblical standards. Furthermore, my generation
enjoyed the benefits of prayer in the school. We even recited
Bible verses and sometimes were asked to pray at the school
my siblings and I attended.

Today, things are different. You have the right to pray on
your own as long as it does not offend others. When I started teaching in the public school system . . . students, parents,
administrators, politicians, and many others would asked me

to pray, especially at a special event. Events like a political election or for a family member's dedication . . . and I would do it without hesitation or question. Times have changed! If I were teaching school today and prayed for someone, I would have to make sure that I did not offend someone due to their religious faith, sexual orientation or belief. Especially, when ending the prayer with "in the name of Jesus." As it relates to marriage, regardless of our upbringing and its influence on marriage stability and longevity, prayer is and always has been the key ingredient. According to an old adage, which is definitely true, says that a "family that prays together will stay together."

Again, it cannot be stressed enough that how we were brought up has a lot to do with the way we treat our spouse and the blueprint for how we will raise our offspring. For example, everybody in my house smoked cigarettes. My mother, my father, my brothers and my sister . . . we all smoked. Where do you think I got the idea? The idea came from family habits and up-bringing. It is the family core values (drinking alcohol, smoking marijuana, use of recreational drugs, sex, pornography, incest, adultery, etc.) that can, later in life, become the reason for unhealthy relating. This dysfunctional relating can lead to divorce, domestic violence and sometimes death.

My problem was that I became a smoker which was influenced by my parents and siblings. Once I realized that smoking was hazardous to my health, I started asking God to take the taste of smoking away from me. It was a struggle because I enjoyed smoking and I thought it was cool.

Finally, I realized that the cigarette does the smoking and I was just a sucker. And God did not intend for me to be a chimney. It took me 16 years to stop smoking completely. Fortunately, my wife and my children never smoked. Therefore, my grandchildren don't have an example of smoking nor drinking from their parents (our children) because, thank God, their grandparents do not smoke.

All of us have some bad habits that we picked up from our upbringing. For some it was smoking, drug and alcohol abuse, or even domestic violence. Fortunately because of the work of Jesus Christ, we don't have to live that way. Always strive to make your marriage the type of relationship God intended. The only way one can overcome bad influences inherited during upbringing is to ask God to help you.

Children: Yours and Mine

Some couples get married with a sole intent on having children, while nature makes the decision for others. Then there are unmarried couples who have children prior to marriage and/or have children by an ex-spouse or companion. Regardless of the reasons, children are a vital part of the family; however, they can be a hindrance to a marriage, if not totally accepted by both spouses.

Whether through divorce or the death of a parent, it is always a crucial period for a child to adjust to a new parent. The younger child appears to better assimilate into a blended family than older children, making it easier and less stressful for a new mother or father. Sometimes it never works out because of the age of the children or due to the new parent finding it difficult to accept or be accepted by the child. Here's some suggestions for what a step parent do in these cases:

(1) be patient with the child in his attempt to adapt to a new environment; (2) put yourself in the child's position because they miss their biological father or mother; (3) don't try to take the place of their biological parent, instead just find your place in their life. Simply being a "buddy" is recommended approach by psychologists; (4) don't try to buy their love with material things; and (5) be patient and let God work things out for you.

Some couples have problems with the biological mother or father visiting the children. Keep in mind when the biological parent visits, it is for the purpose of seeing and spending time with the child and not with you (ex-spouse). Also many problems can arise from a pickup/drop-off of a child. Depending on the meeting place, it can give the impression that you eventually may want to get back together or feel "if it weren't for the child, I would never want to see you again" Don't be prey to such tactics because they can cause more trouble than you realize for both you and the child(ren). Always remember that your child would prefer to have the parents together. Don't mislead them. Once the child accepts the new parent, then, the child will realize that visits from the biological parent is just that...a visit.

Finally, be patient when bringing children into a relationship with new parents. Just like it was with us finding out who we are as newlyweds, the child has to find out who they are with their new parents. Sometimes it takes years for them to make an adjustment, but with perseverance, love, desire and prayer, all things are possible.

THINGS TO DO AND NOT DO

1. Demonstrate love to all of your children, biological or step.

2. Research the person you plan to date or marry.

3. Don't be in a hurry to give in to sex.

4. Treat each child equally; especially when stepchildren are involved.

5. Be willing to make adjustments to someone else's way of living.

6. Be patient! Remember, good things come to those who wait.

7. Don't be so quick to marry when you have unresolved problems of your own.Take care of your baggage before joining with another person.

8. Question a long engagement.

9. Don't start out accepting bad habits that are out of control.

10. Since you are God's best, accept only the best.

Notes - Chapter 3

Notes - Chapter 3

CHAPTER 4
STAGES OF MARRIAGE

I have attended several marriage seminars and workshops that have addressed problems couples have in various stages of their relationship. However, most of the information I received seems to apply to couples regardless of the years they were married or the types of problems they experience.

The stages of marriage apply where you are at the present time. Most seminars address marital problems that can be experienced by to a general audience, not to individual couples. This is the reason why I call this section, the stages of marriage. You'll see what I mean.

Stage 1: 1-5 Years

This is the period which I call *adjustment and familiarity.* It's a stage where you find out who your mate is and become familiar with how things are done and how he or she does them. Another way of putting it is that it is the foundational stage of your marriage because it identifies who you are, where your relationship is, and how to find out what type of marriage will last. These questions may seem logical at first glance, but must be answered if you really want your marriage to work during this stage.

My mother was an employee at Scripto Pen & Pencil Company. Scripto was one of the leading sellers of pens, cigarettes lighters and pencils. In those days they distributed supplies all over the world. However, they didn't have a union. So, students were asked to help picket the company and other businesses that sold Scripto products. Diane and I, both single at the

time, were asked to carry signs in front of Davison's (Macy's) and Riches department stores in downtown, Atlanta, Georgia, to help the employees start their union. Diane and her sister, Shirley, were asked to join the picket line by an employee of Scripto who lived in their community. I was asked to join the group by my mother. This is when Diane and I first met.
Of course, I had a reason to call her house because her sister Shirley was in my group and on occasions I would talk to Diane. Little did we know that we were setup by God to be married a couple years later.

After the Scripto picket line, we continued to talk with each other and began dating. I would soon go away to college. During this time, we communicated by phone while I was away at school, but would spend time together when I came home on breaks. Later, I was drafted into the United States Army and spent a tour of duty in Viet Nam. We were married by the Justice of the Peace in Atlanta and spent only two days together after we got married. After those two days, I did not see her for 14 months.

When we got married, we didn't have a big wedding. We didn't have a cake nor a cupcake. In fact, no pictures were taken, no special guests attended the ceremony and there were no gifts given. We only had each other. So, when I returned from Viet Nam, we were officially married and the first stage of marriage was finally launched.

During this stage you may discover that it's a stage where you finally start to know your mate. While you are single it is so easy to make adjustments when problems arise because you can run home to mother and father. When you repeat those vows at your wedding, things change. The vows you take are sacred vows and should not be taken lightly, but taken seriously because you will be held accountable to God, not to yourself.

In addition, during this stage, there's a "feeling things out" period for each of you; a test to discover what love is all about. There's a big difference between love and love making. It takes a long time to test the validity of love. Love making on the other hand, satisfies sexual thirst for the moment and could be the results of being in love or being in lust. Sometimes, early on, it is difficult to distinguish between the two.

Keep in mind, during this stage that my wife and I were growing up and learning how to be married; we knew that we were in love, but it took years to find out what love is all about. Although I am four years, 17 days, and some minutes older, we didn't debate over our age. Apostle Paul writes:

> *"Love suffers long and is kind: love does not envy; love does not parade itself, is not puffed up; does not behave rudely, does not seek its own, is not provoked, thinks no evil; does not rejoice in iniquity, but rejoices in the truth; bears all things, endures all things"*
> *1 Corinthians 12:4-7.*

Keep in mind, during this stage that my wife and I were growing up and learning how to be married; we knew that we were in love, but it took years to find out what love is all about.

Paul lets us know what unconditional love (agape) is, but to get to that point takes time, patience and commitment from both parties to accomplish such unity expressed in I Corinthians 12. When we got married, both of us encountered temptations from every side. My first teaching job was at a high school in Fayetteville, Georgia; then I worked as an assistant director of bands and band arranger at a local college; I played with a local band in and out of town; and I worked in the public schools as a high school band director. There were temptations from every direction: students, faculty members, parents, and night club goers who did not care if you had on a wedding ring. They did not care whether you were single or married. Women still made attempts to break up our marriage by making suggestions or trying to entice me to break the marriage vows by committing adultery. The band consisted of majorettes, flag members, drill team members, and bannerettes. In some cases, there were at least 60 girls who didn't care if I was an adult or not. In addition, my wife worked at a department store, at a bank in town and in the public school and was invited on occasions to have lunch or dinner with male employees who didn't care that she was married either. Moreover, there were other opportunities that could have caused us to break up, but it did not happen because we knew that we were in love then and now.

These are the temptations I had to endure to make it to the next stage in my marriage. I want you to know, so that you will be prepared when temptations come and how to deal with them. Take me seriously, temptations will come but you can escape. Again Apostle Paul writes:

"No temptation has overtaken you except such as is common to man; but God is faithful, who will not allow you to be tempted beyond what you are able, but with the temptation will also make the way to escape, that you may be able to bear it" 1 Corinthians 10:13.

You can escape temptation if you want to. The problem is that a lot of people enjoy the flings and the one-night stands. During this stage, divorce is vulnerable. That's why many marriages (one in two) may not survive the first year, while others are unable to survive the first three months. Your marriage however, can survive a lifetime when each spouse avoids all kinds of temptation and agree to work through problems.

Stage 2: 6-14 Years

After the first stage, it would seem that nothing can go wrong since you have survived the first five years of marriage. I call this stage, Commit to stay together. Why a commitment to stay together? Staying married with someone for five years should give you a clue what they are about and who she or he really is. I realized that five years was not long enough to determine what my wife liked and disliked about me. Diane worked at the bank and I was a band director at a local high school and worked part-time at one of the colleges in town. My job required a lot of my time since I worked with 155 band members and auxiliary students, parents, fundraising projects, band trips, parades, football games, and activities during school and after school at the high school. In addition, I was a band arranger and assistant director in charge of 200 or more students at the college. As you can see, both of our schedules were full. I had to make the decision not to allow my job to prevent me from staying away from home to much. Therefore, I did not go on out of town trips with the college band.

These events took up a lot of my time away from home. Diane's job schedule was not as rigid as my schedule. However, on occasions she would go out with the women at the bank and sometimes the men who worked there would all meet for happy hour or some other place. I didn't object to her going out every once in a while. However, when it relates to going places with single women, I had something to say about that. The same applies to single men. Their agenda may be different from a married person. Married people have somebody to go home to. Single people are "gamed" to talk and plan other times to meet and get together at other places. For both of us, our jobs and friends took a lot of time away from home and family time. Additionally, Diane and I were drinkers in those days. When she would go out after work, it created problems for us because I had to keep the children and did not know when she would come home. Also I would worry and that either one of us might drink too much and be arrested for drunk driving. God truly blessed us. Fortunately, neither one of us had an accident nor got arrested for breaking the law.

As you can see, we had some problems. We still loved each other, but we were headed in two separate directions. The result of our individual schedules, the drinking, the smoking, the partying, and fussing at each other lead us to consider getting a divorce. We decided to get rid of the house for which we worked hard to purchase. Maybe, that was one of the reasons we were going through the things we were going through. However, both of us knew that divorce was not the answer.

Therefore, we decided to separate instead. We moved in separate apartments to collect ourselves and give time to working things out. Diane's apartment was a block away from mine. It was not planned that way, but that's the way it happened. I helped her move into her apartment and she did the same for me. The move did not effect time at work. Although I had band rehearsals during the summer, school was not in session nor did it have any effect on Diane's job. Moreover, she stopped going out with bank co-workers after we separated. Prior to the separation, some of the female employees had told her that I don't give her space to go places that she wanted to go. In other words, I would not give her opportunity to sin on her own.

Be careful not to listen to people who really need advice themselves. Some of the same people who gave my wife advice about me not giving her opportunity or room to go places on her own, did not ask her for advice when they got married. Their husbands, too, did not agree with them going places with employees at the bank or to going out with friends that were not married.

This stage can be beneficial to your relationship. Single people and married people think differently. People who have children must plan meals and time for the family. We always provided for our children. When we decided to go out, we made sure that our children were in good hands with each other or some other person we could trust. However, as it relates to Diane and me, we learned that our marriage was more important than going out with the boys or the girls. We realized that we could have fun together. Keeping the wrong company can be detrimental to your marriage and cause you never to recover. God saved us from ending our relationship during this stage. I hope you will gain wisdom, knowledge, and understanding of how to avoid some of the pitfalls we entered. Always remember, you can recover from the loss of a house or a car, but if your marriage is worth saving, provisions have been made by God.

Stage 3: 15-25 Years

This stage is the most exciting stage of the five stages. I call this stage *Trusting in the Lord*. During this stage Diane and I discovered that the only way to make our marriage work was to give our lives to Jesus Christ. In fact, when I conduct a marriage ceremony I extend an invitation to the couple to give their lives to the Lord. If they have accepted Christ in their life, then, I marry them.

I am not obligated to marry a couple if I know that they are headed down the wrong road. I know that their marriage will not survive on its own. If they are saved, then, chances are they will have success in the relationship for a long time. Some people may ask, "Why do I need to give my life to Jesus Christ?" The institution of marriage is based on a life of holiness to God and God created marriage. This means being faithful to the Lord and to the one with whom you plan to spend the rest of your life. If you don't think that you have to be faithful to the person that you plan to marry, you will not be obligated to do what's right. We all must be held accountable to someone in authority. In marriage, we must be held accountable to God and love our spouse as Christ loves the church. Paul writes,

> "Husbands, love your wives, just as Christ also loved the church and gave Himself for her, that He might sanctify and cleanse her with the washing of water by the word, that He might present her to Himself a glorious church, not having spot or wrinkle or any such thing, but that she should be holy and without blemish. So husbands ought to love their wives as their own bodies; he who loves his wife loves himself" (Ephesians 5:25-28).

We then, must treat our spouse as Christ treats the church.

The reason why marriages fail is because some couples believe that they should have control over their relationship and should be able to do what they think is right. Eventually you will discover that you don't have all of the answers. When you refuse to do things according to the written word of God, you will find out how little you know about the covenant you entered.

God knows it all. He is all powerful, all knowing, and He is every place at the same time. Don't think that you will not think about sinning by committing adultery or divorcing your spouse and marrying someone else. The wise person will not even think about it, but the folly of fools will do it in a moment's notice. My wife and I thought we were doing just fine when we encountered financial difficulties during this stage; challenges that were similar to the type of problems people are going through today. For example, when my wife was offered a promotion at the bank, it seemed very attractive to her because it offered prestige and an increase in pay. The problem with the promotion was that she would have to spend more time at work. To make a long story short, she refused the offer and was given notice that she would be fired. We thought that she had a very good case for discrimination. The results of her getting fired did not lead to any financial gain from the discrimination suit; she only received money she earned from investing in stocks and her final pay check. This really hurt the family budget since we depended upon both incomes. It set us back, but we didn't give up.

You may remember in Stage 2 that we lost our house, separated, and moved into separate locations. This is how we recovered. We started trusting in the Lord and stop leaning to our own understanding. Solomon writes, "

> *Trust in the Lord with all your heart, and lean not on your own understanding: In all your ways acknowledge Him, and He shall direct your paths" (Proverbs 3:5-6).*

Finally, we started trusting in the Lord. Before then, we only trusted ourselves. Still there's more! After Diane received her final check from the bank, she applied for unemployment compensation. While she was on her way to the unemployment office she had an accident and hit three cars. One of the cars was a classic automobile. The drivers of the three cars she hit were very helpful and tried to comfort her and make sure that she was alright. When she called me she was crying and very upset because of what had happened. I gave her encouragement that everything would be alright. Then she told me that she cancelled the insurance on the car because we needed money to pay for bills and provide for the family. When she said that, then I wanted to cry, too. Fortunately, we survived the obstacles we faced and were able to live on the money I received from my job.

After we joined the church and began to depend on the Lord as our source for everything, I applied for the position as commander of the Georgia Army National Guard Band. I was told by a minister at the church we attended that if I give my life to the Lord and Savior Jesus Christ, I would receive the position as commander of the band. Needless to say, I questioned as to why I had to give my life to Jesus. Nevertheless, after I gave my life to the Lord, I passed the test and fulfilled all of the requirements to receive the rank of WO1, commander of the Georgia Army National Guard band. I held the position as commander of the band until I was called into the ministry two years later.

This drew us closer to each other more than ever before. We realized that it was nothing that we had done. Therefore, we give all of the praise, the glory, and the honor to the author and finisher of our faith, the Lord Jesus Christ. If you put your trust in Him, you will discover that what He did for our relationship, He will do for your marriage too.

Stage 4: 26-43 Years

I call this stage *Maturing Together*. During this stage, strange things can happen in your relationship. We survived 26 years of success in marriage. However, some people might say at this point: "it's cheaper to keep her "and "it's too late to turn back now", or "it's either now or never" and "you better shop around". Those phrases were also used in songs years ago.

Listen, people will also try to use these themes in their present stage of marriage. In other words, some people realize that they are getting older and the school boy or school girl figure has disappeared forever, they feel their need to recapture it and resort to the following:

1. Have a face lift
2. Change their hair style
3. Lose weight
4. Date and have an affair with someone younger
5. Hang out with the younger crowd
6. Do things you always wanted to do

This approach does not solve the problem of getting old. Nor does it make or diminish your relationship with your spouse. Regardless of the stage, marriage should be honorable and enjoyable.

We must realize that we are going to get older and our marriage will not end because of our age. Getting older is a reason to stay together for life. God has placed you with the one He wants you to be with so that you may grow old together and enjoy each other for life. If one spouse should depart before the other, let God decide what the surviving spouse should do. Paul writes,

> "For I wish that all men were even as I myself. But each one has his own gift from God, one in this manner and another in that. But I say to the unmarried and to the widows: It is good for them if they remain even as I am; but if they cannot exercise self-control, let them marry. For it is better to marry than to burn with passion"
> (1 Corinthians 7:7-9).

Paul sums it up by letting us know a way to go should we be prematurely separated from our spouse by death and find ourselves needing a companion. However, if we are still alive, marriage is still just as honorable as it was during the first stage.

Stage 5: 44 Years to Life

Stage 5 is what I call We *Made it through*. Now that you have become aware of the stages of marriage, what will you do now? I suggest that you consider where you are in your relationship and do all you can to make it last. <u>Unfortunately, today, couples are divorcing after being married much longer than my wife and I have been married</u>. Diane and I struck gold when we found each other. Others may have looked and found "fools gold" and have not profited at all. I suggest that you take your time and be wise in your selection of a mate. Good things come to those who wait. Therefore, I say to you, Wait!

Be encouraged to be led by the living God who is able to cause your marriage to prosper. Only you can make it work. I can only give suggestions for that which has worked for Diane and me, during each of these stages. Beyond the list of suggestions that have definitely worked in our marriage, it is the responsibility of each spouse to consider and take note of what worked for us. I believe that if you adhere to them, your marriage can last 40 years and longer.

Notes - Chapter 4

Notes - Chapter 4

CHAPTER 5
CONFLICTS AND RESOLUTIONS

Most people are not aware of the meaning of conflict resolution. They confuse conflict with disagreement, stress, and simple experiences that may cause a conflict, but do not justify the true meaning of the word.

Daniel Dana defines conflict by listing their four causes:
- (1) Interdependence
- (2) Blaming each other
- (3) Anger
- (4) Behavior that causes business problems.

These four causes are an excellent guideline you can use to determine whether you and your spouse are in conflict with each other. If you know what the problem is, chances are you can find a solution.

Sometimes people fight over trivial matters and allow problems to linger unresolved for a long period of time, then, they forget how the problems started. They bicker over things they can't remember and remain angry at one another. This is the main reason couples need to know how to deal with conflict.

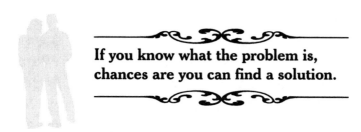

**If you know what the problem is,
chances are you can find a solution.**

Sex, Communication and Money

This section deals with the three most important subjects that cause marriages to end. One popular radio and television personality said that money is the number one reason why couples break up. In my opinion, communication is the number one cause of break ups. Money is a necessity to be used to fulfill the needs for the household. Communication must be prevalent whether you have money or not. You need to communicate how to get money, but communication is essential regardless of your financial status. On the matter of sex, it will not be as enjoyable as it should be when one wants it and the other does not, but he or she does it to satisfy the other. Otherwise, having sex without communicating becomes legal prostitution because you do it to please the money giver and not yourself. Therefore, communication is one of the major reasons marriages end in divorce.

Edwin Louis Cole did a series on sex, communication and money in 1989. This series blessed so many people who did not know how to deal with problems they faced in their marriage. I used the information to share with friends to assist them in building relationships. This section deals with ways to prevent marriages from breaking up.

Sex

Among the three headings in this section, sex is the one that's not so easy to be forgiven. Some people treat sex as a selfish act of control that enables them to have it with whom they choose and at anytime they want. It may be a one night stand with someone or someone may become a mistress for life. They rely on promises rarely fulfilled. Others may accept an invitation from someone they just met and have sex without question, not considering the consequences that may lead to divorce or the catching of a disease that could lead to death.

Finally, others cherish sex as an honor to have it with the one they love and make every effort not to violate trust or disappointment.

Anyone who is having sex outside of marriage does not have respect for their spouse. And whether you realize it or not, the other one knows that something is not right in the relationship. It's that mother's wit that women particularly have. Some people are bold enough to live as an invited guest in your home with you and your spouse and will have sex with either spouse. Don't make it a habit of allowing people to stay with you even in emergency cases. Find another way to help them. In addition, don't give permission for someone to visit you when you are not at home. Your mate might wonder why you allowed him or her to enter your home in both your absence. The best way to solve this problem is never allow it to happen.

I was very proud of my wife when a local band director came to my house to pick up music I arranged for his school band. My wife told him that I was not at home and he would have to wait outside until I came home. Sure enough, when I came home, she told me that the director came to pick up the arrangement and she did not invite him in. When I came home and looked outside, I discovered that he was waiting for me in his car. My wife knew what to do in this situation. You may say that it is not necessary to take such precautions. How do you know? Give no room to seductive spirits. If you don't give in, there's nothing to be obtained.

Always remember, sex is still as active in the last stage of marriage as it is in the first stage. The biggest difference is that the quantity of times you have it is not as important as the quality of the times.

Communication

This topic is the number one problem couples have in their relationship whether single or married. The problem is communication. Communication is defined as the means of sending and receiving of messages. To communicate is difficult in most cases because some people have a lot to say, but don't know how to say it.

It was easy when Diane and I first met because we had a lot in common. She played the flute and I played the trumpet. In addition, she thought that she knew more about music than I until she discovered that I was majoring in music in college. She was amazed at the amount of knowledge I had on the subject of music. Moreover, she played in Archer High School band in Atlanta where they thought that they had the best band in the land. I played in Tennessee State University Aristocrats of bands and she knew that we were among the best in those days. So, we had a lot in common and it was very easy to express our feelings. That made it easy for me to get my point of view across to her and vice versa. She had a voice to express what she had to say, and so did I. Problems occurred, however, when we got into an argument, or talked about things we thought were so easy to share, but we did not know how to communicate. So, we clashed because one of us wanted to dominate the conversation, and because we did not know how to work together in conversing with each other, we stopped talking.

I recall during the first stage of my marriage how long it took us to make up and start back talking. We went from several days, to a day, to an hour, and finally to a minute before we started talking again. The funny thing about it was we stopped talking to each other over something trivial that we disagreed about from watching the television, or listening to the radio, believing what someone said about the other, or even had differences of opinion. How did we solve the problem? Well . . . we knew that if neither one talked, both of us had a problem. It didn't matter who caused the problem, the goal was to find a way to start us communicating again. In other words, regardless of the reason why we stop talking, both of us are obligated to make every effort to work things out.

The solution is to continue communicating even if it hurts to say something nice. I guarantee you'll be grateful you made the first move. You must work through it regardless what has happened. At the end, you will be amazed how trivial matters can stop you from expressing the love you have for your mate. The next time a problem arises, it will only take a minute to work it out.

Money

Years ago, the husband or father was the one who provided for the family. He was the only one working in the house and the sole breadwinner. Today, both parents work cooperatively to provide for the household. Sometimes the mother makes more money than the father. If the mother makes more money than the father, it can cause problems because some men think that women should make a lower salary than men. Times have changed. Some females make more money than men because they are just as qualified as men and deserve the pay. Both parents should be willing to combine their income to foster financial stability and have a better way of life for their families.

The problem with women making more money than men is not the biggest problem. When both have separate bank accounts, buy their own car, buy their clothes and supply just enough money to insure that all of the bills are paid, eventually, they are going to have more problems than they can handle.

Where there's unity, there's strength. We believe that there should only be one checking account and one savings account in both names. The charge cards should be in both names also. If you attend church and believe in tithing, you should write one check for tithes and offering. This demonstrates oneness in the relationship. The reasons for these inclusions are to give the woman just as much right to various accounts and cards as the man. Also, if something should happen to either spouse, the other spouse has access to all accounts and other business matters. This makes it easy to operate the family budget in case of an emergency.

In addition, some people don't want to purchase a large life insurance policy for fear that the spouse will use the money for the wrong purpose. This should not be a problem for the beneficiary spouse because he or she must do what is right for the children and self. When money is used for the entire house, God blesses the family. If we decide not to put our money together, we open the door to be cursed for not trusting God. The bottom line is to make every effort to live as a family by putting all of the money together and living as one unit. By doing so, you have all things in common and will keep the channel of community open for success.

REACHING LEADERS in the MINISTRY

Most people come to marriage seminars for the purpose of receiving healing and repair of their relationships. Lay people respond without hesitation. On the other hand, the clergy and other church leaders are the hardest to reach. The reason why they don't respond as quickly as lay people is beyond me. Perhaps they don't want others to see that they have weaknesses like everybody else. Without immediate attention, the problem continues to linger and cause more heartaches, misunderstandings, and apathy that can eventually lead to divorce.

Nevertheless, some people carry their problems over to the next seminar and never get healed. The problems they face will continue to escalate unless they admit that they too, have problems.

Today, so many people in the ministry are getting divorce because they have come to the conclusion that the only way to solve their marital problems is to end their relationship.

There are two factors or fallacies: (1) Qualified counselors may exist, but often unavailable to minister to them; and (2) Married couples feel that they can solve their own problems.

There are so many qualified people who can minister to you and your spouse. If you are looking for someone with outstanding counseling credentials; that may not be the person God will use to help you. On the other hand, if you are looking for someone who is in the body of Christ for help, you may limit available resources and take the wrong approach.

However, if you trust God to fix your problems, He will send you someone you don't know, a person without a well known reputation, someone not known in the community or around the world, but a person sent by God under the anointing to tell you the truth, what you need to do, how to do it, and advise you to follow God's instructions to save your marriage.

Sometimes the problem is you. Receiving the best help is not always easy to find. In some cases, well-known ministers have contact with well-known people, but they may not be the best people you need to resolve your conflicts. In fact, it would be better if you didn't use these types of people. God is the only one who can determine the most qualified person for you and your spouse.

For example, when my wife and I searched for assistance for help with our marital problems, we went to a marriage counselor outside of the church. Although we were not saved at the time, it worked just as well as it would have been if we had being ministered to by someone skilled in the counseling profession. We were led by God to go to the marriage counselor that He sent us to. You must use your best judgment in determining what's best for your situation.

The second factor, "We can solve our own problems", can be very risky. If you could resolve your marital problems, there would be no need for a mediator. In most situations, the problem was caused by both spouses. If married couples think they can solve their own problem, that's great. This kind of conflict resolution between married couples only happens when such couples are experienced and are aware of Satan's tactics; so both parties actively practice communicating to reconcile their differences . . . regardless of the time or cost involved. This is rare and in most cases they end up seeking help from an experienced counselor. It's risky because you could make matters worse. Experienced couples understand why they are married and the price to stay married. However, just knowing what it takes to stay together and maintain happiness is not enough. The ultimate goal is to love each other as Christ loves the Church, and make every effort to treat your spouse as if he /she is Christ Himself.

To the hard- to-reach people, always seek help when you know that you cannot handle the situation. None of us have all of the answers. Don't ever forget, if you want to work things out, you can. If one side doesn't feel that the two of you can work things out, it won't be worked out.

LET'S KISS and MAKE UP

Out of the 44 years of misunderstandings, disappointments, the anger, the heartaches, and the pain, whether my fault or Diane's, we can't list the problems that were not worth making up...or worth breaking up over. It is very difficult to live with someone and continue to be irate. There must be a pause at some point to say" I am sorry . . . honey let's make up". How do you do it? Diane and I simply said "I am sorry and I love you". I encourage you to say something sweet. It always helps. Don't let a day pass by without resolving a problem. Apostle Paul writes,

> *"Be angry, and do not sin": do not let the sun go*
> *down on your wrath, nor give place to the devil,"*
> *Ephesians 4:26, 27).*

He was right when he said don't go to sleep mad at each other. Instead, make up before you go to bed. You will have a renewed relationship in the morning. Otherwise, the problems will continue to snowball rather than find a solution.

There are several ways to express feelings and make up: buy a gift or take a trip, prepare a hand-made or printed card and give flowers along with it. But let me tell you, the best way to make up is to kiss. Gifts will work most of the time. Remember, the best things in life are free. Kiss and make up.

THINGS TO DO AND NOT DO

1. If it takes two to cause a conflict, be the first one to resolve it.

2. Don't wait until a new problem arrives, then, bring up unresolved issues.

3. All couples love to have sex . . . is it the right time for both of you?

4. Tell your spouse when you are overdrawn on your checking account.

5. Set a financial budget and stick to it.

6. Don't leave a marriage seminar without getting your needs met.

7. Don't limit help to Christian counselors to resolve conflicts.

8. Don't leave home without a kiss.

9. If it causes problems, let the other spouse manage the finances.

10. Don't let a day go by without making up.

Notes - Chapter 5

Notes - Chapter 5

CHAPTER 6
MAINTAINING A HEALTHY RELATIONSHIP

How Can Married Couples Make It Last?

If you value your marriage, it means you have made every effort to maintain it. Just because a conflict or a misunderstanding occurs, it does not mean that it is time to throw in the towel. A marriage is worth saving, especially when it has been bombarded with only trivial issues. These are tactics Satan use to cause separation and or divorce.

A healthy marriage will face tests, trials and victories. The good news is that we can overcome any obstacle that Satan throws at us. Apostle Peter writes,

> *"Beloved do not think it strange concerning the fiery trial which is to try you, as though some strange thing happened to you: but rejoice to the extent that you partake of Christ's sufferings, that when His glory is revealed, you may also be glad with exceeding joy"* (1 Peter 4:12 – 13).

Diane and I rejoice in the fact that we are still together. The trials we have experienced did not cause us to quit loving each other or walk away from our marriage vows – for better or worse, and in sickness and health, etc.

A marriage is worth saving, especially when it has been bombarded with only trivial issues

The first thing to do is to realize that problems will come and go. How spouses deal with their problems will determine relationship longevity. The longer your marriage exists, experience will remind you that certain kinds of situations have happened before. What should be done about it? Don't panic! It's a test. Married couples can now pass the test by solving marital problems as they occur. Don't allow your spouse's concern to get out of hand by ignoring it and doing nothing about it. All matters need each spouse's immediate attention.

Your marriage will survive a lifetime, if you will maintain it with care. If a spouse decides to let matters get out of hand, their nonchalant behavior and lack of spousal respect will not allow the marriage to last.

Diane and I realized long ago that if we decided to never make up, we would lose each other. Obviously, we agreed that we didn't want that to happen. We were willing to forget all of the things we heard, things we said, and things we did that may have hurt or embarrassed each other, but we were willing to forget all of those things to get back together. That's what you have to do to make it last. Just don't take someone else's word regarding conflict without wise counsel. Get the facts. You are the carrier of the successes and failures that steer a marriage in the right direction and make it last a lifetime. Take advantage of it . . . and act on it.

Learn from our experiences. When Diane and I got married I did not help wash dishes nor clean up the house, or involve myself with tasks I thought were traditionally handled by women. I've changed and now do my part to help out. To make the marriage last, you may have to perform tasks you never imagined doing. Handling these are the kinds of things that will definitely help make your marriage last, and the list should come from each spouse.

There is nothing written that says you are restricted from performing tasks traditionally handled by women, i.e. doing laundry, cooking or grocery shopping, even combing the children's hair for school. Everybody in the household has a job to do. The most important job a husband and wife must perform is to do all they can to live in peace and to love each other just as Christ loves the Church. The ability to keep peace will maintain a healthy environment and lasting relationship. When we do all that we can do to cause our marriage to succeed, we will make it last forever.

Growing Together and Not Apart

When I met my wife I was a senior in college majoring in music education. My plans after graduation were to pursue a master of music degree and to work in a position at a high school as a band teacher. However, I changed my mind because I applied too late for a teacher's position in Atlanta and was drafted into the U.S. Army.

I became interested in band music when I was in elementary school watching bands in parades. During those years, high school bands would pass by my house twice a year. So, I developed a love for the trumpet and made music my career.

I did further study to receive a master of music and worked at a local college and retired from the public school. In addition, I received another master's degree and a doctorate degree and did further study in religion and education.

On the other hand, my wife attended college only one year. I was drafted into the Army and spent a tour of duty in Viet Nam. We got married before I left for Viet Nam. After we got married, as stated earlier, we were together only two days; then, I had to return to Fort Mead, Maryland to prepare to deploy for

Viet Nam. I returned home after completing 11 months in Viet Nam. Sadly, I was not home when my daughter was born. The bottom line is that my wife did not have the opportunity to continue going to college while I was in the Army because we could not afford to send her to school and she was raising our daughter.

After I completed my time in the Army, we had to stay with my parents until we got adjusted and was able to afford our own residence.

After all of those years of studying and receiving more education, it did not conflict with her deciding not to continue her education. Instead, Diane worked in the school system as a senior secretary for the principal; a head teller at the bank, a title examiner and worked on other jobs that assisted her in knowing how to manage the school's office and make quick decisions and assist faculty and staff personnel. Although our educational backgrounds are different, we never thought that either one was better than the other.

Moreover, my wife has always thought she was smarter than I am; she came to her senses when she realized that she made a wise choice in selecting me as a husband. And so did I in choosing her as my wife.

Diane has always communicated very well with people with extensive scholastic backgrounds without embarrassment or intimidation. She has always handled herself appropriately and expressed herself when it was necessary to communicate with others.

On the other hand, some people grow apart when one spouse receives more education than the other. Example, one spouse, promises to help the other spouse obtain a college education with the understanding that after he or she graduates from college he or she would help the other complete their education. In some cases, this never happens. The reason for this may be because one decided not to go to school; they couldn't afford it; or they used the money for some other reason.

When one spouse sets goals to further their education or pursue another career choice without considering the growth of the other spouse, you may start growing apart. Goal setting should be the goal for the couple. We never stop planning for a better way of life. Sometimes we become complacent and think that our plans are secure for life. Moreover, we never stop setting higher goals.

Years ago, retirement meant working to age 65. After that time, you were considered retired. Your retirement pay was sufficient enough to last for the rest of your life. Today, companies don't provide medical care, dental care or retirement benefits sufficient enough to last for the rest of your life. Social security and other financial savings are no longer enough to care for you and your family as long as you live. Let's face it, the economy of the Unites States has diminished and is still decreasing to the level that there is no such thing as retirement. Therefore, unless you have tremendous amounts of investments and savings, you may have to consider working well after retirement age.

To grow together and not grow apart, one must consider the entire family. Your children need to set wise goals for a better life. The preparation for this should start early. They must be encouraged to study hard, make good grades and make the right choices now and not to wait until it's too late.

Selecting a career is very important. However, just choosing a career that you really like is not always the best decision. Computer technology, the medical profession, law enforcement, just to name a few, only works when you know without a shadow of doubt that these careers will last. Nevertheless, you may have to change careers during your tenure at your present job to prepare for the future.

Today, there are no occupations that will last until retirement. The education profession will last for a long time. However, in certain school systems across America, teachers and administrators are asked to take furloughs because of cuts in the school system's budgets. Some people lose their job so the school system can make the budget.

When your children plan to secure their future or leave home to live on their own, this takes financial pressure off parents. Only when there is an emergency need to help your children should your support be extended to them.

Married people must stay focused on the oath they took at the altar. "In sickness and in health, to love and to cherish, until we are parted by death; as God is my witness, I give you my promise." This is so easy to say, but to live it necessitates willingness to stay together and not separate from each other is the ultimate challenge. Not every couple is able to accomplish such goals, but it is worth the time and effort to try hard each day to make it happen.

Our goal should be to try to recapture and maintain the enjoyment we've experienced over the years, every day of our lives together. A new hair style, new clothes, and staying physically fit will help make the sparks last in a loving relationship. However, to keep us from growing apart, it's up to us.

THINGS TO DO AND NOT DO

1. Don't wait until it is too late to share concerns with your spouse.

2. Make a special effort to keep your relationship from failing.

3. Never think you are too old to go back to school.

4. Never stop setting goals.

5. Don't think you are inferior for lack of education.

6. Plan now for retirement regardless of your age.

7. Grow together by looking good, feeling good, and being good to each other.

8. Don't think it's too late to change your career.

9. Repeat your marriage vows to each other and maintain them.

10. Make a special effort not to grow apart.

Notes - Chapter 6

EPILOGUE

Marriage is still the best way to live a healthy life. Not only do you have the privilege to live with someone you love, but also to accept the challenge of fulfilling the sacred vows you made before God and man, honoring a plan that God established before the foundation of the world.

However, the enjoyment and longevity of marriage does not come easy without dedication, sacrifice, hard work and determination. One couple may find it easy to live together and overlook current obstacles without solving their problems. Another couple may discover after getting married that marriage is not what they thought it would be. Because of these reasons, some of them take the divorce route. Still others may find ways of dealing with the temptations and disappointments, the trials and errors; and despite it all, refuse to give up their relationship without a fight. The real reason is that they love each other and are willing to find ways to solve their problems.

I often wonder what I would have done without my wife. I am sure I would have found someone to spend my life with, but not like the one I fell in love with. Fortunately, when I found my wife I knew I'd better move expeditiously and marry her without delay. Why? Let's face it, there is no guaranteed that your mate will wait until you decide to get married. However, this does not mean that you should not wait for the best candidate.

"The Lord is good to those who wait for Him"
(Lamentations 3:25).

For me, a marriage without kids would have been incomplete. (If you can't have children of your own due to medical reasons, you might consider adoption. There are many children in the world who would love to be in your family.) The good part about it is that when Diane and I get older, we will have two children and grandchildren who are obligated to share their love for us and look out for us because we are bonded together for life. They don't have to take care of us unless we can't provide for each other, but the Word of God says,

"Train up a child in the way he should go, And when he is old he will not depart from it" (Proverbs 22:6).

This tells me that my children depended on me and my wife for their well being when they were young, and when they become old they will depend on their children to watch over them. Therefore, having children is great but training children the way they should go after they become adults is a reflection of how we were raised.

However, the parental role modeling job is not as easily forecasted. First of all, there are more temptations than ever before; people are getting divorced earlier and more than ever; couples are living together and having children; and others are marrying the same sex. These factors are among the list of reasons people don't get married and stay married.

God! Please Save My Marriage is a testimony of the potential problems couples face in finding ways to stay together. It is not an easy task. When I got married I tried to follow my parents' examples and other people I knew who appeared to be happily married. I had no idea what challenges I would face in the future. The good news is that marriage was and still is an honorable institution in the sight of God and should not be entered into without a serious commitment to stay together for life.

Staying married can only be done with the assistance of the Holy Spirit of God.

If you don't know the Holy Spirit, I guarantee you before long you will find out that He is the one who can do all things, especially when it comes to keeping things in order.

Conflicts, money, misunderstandings, and infidelity can be resolved. The Bible says that we are to forgive each other seventy times seven. Apostle Matthew writes that Apostle Peter came to Him (Jesus) and said,

> *"Lord, how often shall my brother sin against me, and I forgive him, up to seven times?" Jesus said to him, "I do not say to you, up to seven times, but up to seventy times seven" (Matt 18:21,22).*

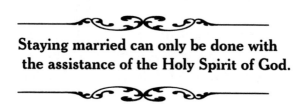

Staying married can only be done with the assistance of the Holy Spirit of God.

The Lord set a standard for forgiveness that goes beyond our standard of forgiveness. In other words, our relationship should be so fine-tuned that we are willing to forgive each other up to 490 times a day. If you want your marriage to work, and work, and continue to work, you must be willing to forgive and forget and continue to forgive.

Problems should be admitted and acquitted. Thrown into the sea of forgetfulness and not mentioned anymore. I forgive you and you forgive me. Every time you follow this format, you start over again. This is the key to an everlasting relationship. Always willing to make up and not break up.

The devil will try to encourage you to throw in the towel and say your marriage was not intended to last. That's a lie! If that was the truth, why did you get married in the first place? If God put you together, you made the right choice. Now "let's stay together", as Al Green once said.

The 44 years that Diane and I have been together is the result of God's forgiveness and our ability to forgive each other. If you ask Him, God can save and repair your marriage, too.

There are only two types of marriages:
(1) Between a man and a woman; and
(2) Between Christ and the Church.

God ordained for man and woman to be joined together for life, to love one another, and to be fruitful and multiply. Moses writes,

"So God created man in His image; male and female He created. Then God blessed them, and God said to them, be fruitful and multiply; fill the earth and subdue it; have dominion over the fish of the sea, over the birds of the air, and over every living thing that moves on the earth" (Genesis 1:27, 28).

It has always been God's desire for man and woman to be joined together. Today, some people don't think that marriage is the answer for companionship. They prefer living together and consider marriage as a thing of the past. I beg the difference. God's desire for every man is for him to have his own wife. It was God's plan then and it is His plan now.

The second type of marriage will take place at the marriage supper of the Lamb. When Jesus returns for His church, we will become married to Him. At the present time, we are engaged to the Lord. Apostle John the Beloved and dearest friend to Our Lord and Savior Jesus Christ writes,

> *"Let us be glad and rejoice and give Him glory, for the marriage of the Lamb has come, and His wife has made herself ready." And to her it was granted to be arrayed in fine linen, clean and bright, for the fine linen is the righteous acts of the saints" (Revelation 19:7-9).*

Finally, of all the things I learned about marriage, the one thing that will not be superseded by anything is prayer. My wife and I found out what marriage is all about when we started praying for each other and depending upon God for everything. We do this every day.

The following is a model prayer that can be used daily to support your marriage in any situation:

Pray this simple prayer with your spouse:

Father, help us to keep our marriage healthy, faithful and enjoyable all the days of our lives. We know that we will have problems, but there are no problems You cannot solve. Teach us to always come to You when we need help in our marriage. We will always remember that there is no problem you cannot solve. Lord, teach us how to forgive and forget and not to bring up things that causes conflicts, but rather help us to say and do things that are beneficial for each other's growth and prosperity. Help us to realize that all things are possible to them that believe and trust in You. Thank you Father God for hearing our prayer and healing our marriage in Jesus' name . . . Amen.

SCRIPTURAL INDEX

ABOUT THE AUTHOR

Dr. Robert E. Flournoy and his wife Diane were ordained in Hampton, Georgia, in 1989. He holds the Bachelors of Science degree in Music Education, the Master of Music degree, the Master of Divinity and the Doctor of Ministry degrees. Moreover, he holds a T-5 and an Instructional Supervision certificate for life in the state of Georgia. He is a retired teacher (director of bands) in the Atlanta Public Schools and served as the commander of the Georgia Army National Guard Band. In addition, he taught and arranged music for colleges and high schools throughout the southeast and served as the Chairman of the Ethics Commission for the Clayton County Board of Education.

In 1989, Dr. Flournoy and his wife founded the Divine House of Praise Church in Atlanta, Georgia. They are overseers of Divine House of Praise and the Prophetic Anointing International Ministries. He and Diane are Father and Mother of nine Ministries. They have two children and two grandchildren and make their home in Jonesboro, Georgia.

His book, *God! Please Save My Marriage* is his first book to go to press. In the very near future, he will complete his next book, Instant Increase in the Anointing.

For further information and contact for workshops and speaking engagements, please call or email Dr. Flournoy at: 404-366-4635 and drref@bellsouth.net

Notes

Notes

Notes

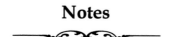

Notes

CPSIA information can be obtained at www.ICGtesting.com
Printed in the USA
LVOW05s1301250214

375088LV00003B/60/P